Your words are worthy.
Your voice is important.

PUBLISH HER HARDCOVER JOURNAL

Printed in the United States of America

Published by Publish Her, LLC
6726 Walker Street
St. Louis Park, MN 55426
www.publishherpress.com

Publish Her is a female-founded publisher dedicated to educating authors and elevating the words, stories and writing of women.

www.ingramcontent.com/pod-product-compliance
Ingram Content Group UK Ltd.
Pitfield, Milton Keynes, MK11 3LW, UK
UKHW021959270726
14060UKWH00003B/595